The E

The Anatomy of The Honey Bee

The Honey Bee (*Apis mellifera*) is a eusocial.

Her womb runs the hive.

It is her eggs that will spawn the hive's next generation of bees.

The honey bee can only sting once.

When she stings you,

her lancets become embedded in your skin.

Remember,

This Bee does not sting for fun.

They do so only when they feel threatened

or

in defense of their *nests*.

It is scientifically proven that the Honey Bee will protect her home at the risk of her own life.

To Evelyn,

I will protect you at the risk of every life that I ever live.

And to everyone else who forgot how to use their wings:

The sky

still

tastes like honey.

Fly.

Introduction

In May 2018, I accomplished one of my biggest dreams: I graduated from Harvard Law School at twenty-four. We crossed the stage to accept our Juris Doctor with tears of relief (and disbelief) streaming down my face. I did not achieve it alone; therefore, I refused to walk unless Harvard allowed me to carry my other, even bigger dream with me: Evelyn Willow. We did it.

"Single Mother Graduates Harvard Law School at 24" circulated the web for months afterwards. Interview requests from multiple large media platforms and frequent questions from my newly-gained social media following flooded my inboxes. Searching for inspiration in my triumphs, the world was a stampede that came knocking at the door of my celebration to demand I share with them a formula that I didn't even know the ingredients to. Everyone needed to know one thing: *how*?

How did I do it? My 150-odd, glamour-filled Instagram posts were enough of a distraction for people to praise my "effortless journey." Overnight, I'd branded myself as a life-coach. I became an expert in law, finances, and motherhood amongst other things. Using my platform to motivate others is how I stayed relevant. I struggle(d) to offer non-cliche insight into thousands of strangers' daily problems.

Telling people how to overcome battles that I, myself, still struggle with quickly became tiring. I found myself caught at the crossroads of flattery and guilt. I questioned my identity and compared her to who I am in your eyes.

You'd be surprised at how much pain we harbor in secret. We can fool one another. We can dress ourselves in success and happiness, so much that people envy everything we have. And beneath the validation of all of those "likes" and "comments," our injustices, abuse, and pain remain unconfronted, slowly unraveling.

With this in mind, I've decided to give you the most reliable formula that I can: truth. I hope you didn't come here looking for my assurance of your happy-ending. I will not give that to you, because I do not have yours. This is not your hiding place.

You are holding my diary in your hands. These are my entries throughout law school, during my pregnancy, my first love, and my heartbreak. These pages hold my deepest secrets. They recount some of my darkest hours, happening during the best times of my life. They were not written with you in mind, and they will not fake the parts of my success story that may make you uncomfortable. I hope by now you've realized that there is no formula except for the one that you already have. I hope you also realize that you are not alone.

If you will take anything at all from me, let it be this:

Life can only give to you what you take from it.

With each sting, I always decide to take the Honey.

Now I'm the Honey-maker (Mellifera).

Part I- Broken Hive

Beloved, have we stung one another beyond the depths of reconciliation?

Oct. 17, 2018: The Honey Bee (The End)

I had to let Evelyn's dad go if I wanted to survive. We were war-zone lovers. We introduced one another to the worst sides of ourselves, and those demons consummated as such so that pain tasted like ecstasy. Two decaying bodies who thought we were happy. Our only true commitment was the interchangeable union of love and hate that we'd wed ourselves to. I could not tell you the difference between passion and possession, but what I could tell you was that I was not going to let that man go. I wanted total control. I needed him at my mercy. He ignited a passion in me that I never knew could exist; therefore, I wanted to own his soul like he owned my sanity.

In the end, we stood across from one another barricaded in the damage that we'd created. Shattered egos, broken promises, severed family ties: a future of ruins. We held guns to each other's head. Love was written on the barrels, but it no longer felt good. Neither of us would have even noticed if Evelyn was part of our war.

I pressed the trigger first.

I had to protect my home. I had to protect Evelyn.

His final breath hummed like rustic saxophone notes. I bawled uncontrollably, all the way to his lion-like carcass.

Instead of resuscitating him, I reached deep into his rib cage. I knew that's where he'd been hiding my wings.

I walked away accepting that my home had been destroyed.

But at least I have the potential to fly again.

Teach Them How You Treat You

Why do you expect

the games to end

when you're still playing your part?

April 2, 2016- Positive (2)

Cinco de Mayo 2016

Planned Parenthood

9 weeks, 0 days

0 days

When I got tired of dressing in lust

for ghoulish lovers

and friends with flesh like idolatry,

I found your father.

I made the decision to be Naked for him.

He devised a trail of petals whose scent would lead me astray.

I thought we were going to pray together,

in his garden.

It left my skin raw, the way I scavenger hunted for him to find a way to love me.

I searched every moon.

And like the sweetest nectar and pollen,

you were my reward.

You were a divine find,

my holy souvenir.

I miss you cannot describe the way that

"You are missing from me."

I pray to you for forgiveness more than I've asked God.

I spend weeks inside of my head creating worlds where you still exist.

In our world, we have erased the sound of that suction—the hum of a thousand bees that came with the sting of a thousand more.

I pick every sunflower on earth and offer you them for your hair.

For each of your baths, I drain every ocean in the solar system.

You wear the sun as a brooch.

I sketch your smile, and it replaces the entire New Testament.

I leave notes in your palm:

"There is an

Infinite bed of lilacs

Waiting for you,

inside of me.

Please come back."

RX

You ache to be healed

By the (lost) one that broke you.

The fact that they so easily

Cut soul ties with your loyalty

Shows you that they cannot give you

Remedies that they may never know.

They can't heal themselves.

8:32 a.m.

June 7, 2016

On April 2, 2016, I found out that I was pregnant. I'd had suspicions...Very vivid dreams of a baby girl. I felt like I had the flu. I was extremely sweaty all the time. The thought of red wine (my favorite) repulsed me, and everyone smelled like shit. I was constantly sleep deprived, my skin was greasier, and walking around Cambridge—actually just walking in general—made me feel like I wanted to jump out of my skin.

I hadn't thoroughly thought it through. It was a spontaneous, heat-of-the-moment kind of "gesture". It was not the idea of being a mother, but the idea of carrying his child—something that belonged to him— that flushed me feverishly. To hear him mention the possibility of us having a family, all the while my breasts aching, my lower back burning, and my stomach cramping with fire gave me a sense of belonging. Hope. Gave me a new challenge—something that I felt I'd been missing for the longest.

So there I was, lying in bed all day, listening to the music boxes lodged in his throat as he constantly suggested that I was pregnant (he thought he knew because he was sleepy all the time (this is a southern folklore and he is from Georgia)). I somewhat believed him, but I didn't want to feed into it because I am the MOST dramatic person in the world and didn't want to have false hope. But, on April 2nd, I was craving smoothies (strawberry banana) more than ever, so I walked all the way to Harvard Square to satisfy that "I MUST have" craving. Turns out Liquiteria was closed, so I hiked to CVS and grabbed a Bolthouse Farm drink...or it may have been a Naked smoothie...Just know that it was some generic, sugary shit that you're really not supposed to consume, especially if you're (possibly?) preggo, lol.

Anyways, I'm standing in the artificial food aisle and it occurs to me that maybe I should go and buy a pregnancy test. We'd planned to take it together on my next trip to see him, but I was curious. I could never stand the unknown. I went upstairs (the CVS has two stories) and picked up a Clear Blue digital test box: the kind that comes with two, just in case you don't believe your eyes, I suppose. When I left the store, I ran into a friend whose liquor-stained breath made me all but run to the toilet. Upon arrival to the toilet (finally) I took the test.

Lo and behold, it was positive (both times because I couldn't believe my eyes, I suppose).

That was the day that part of me came alive.

That was the day that part of me died.

The Greatest Lie Ever Told

My reactions don't define me.

Don't you dare use my brokenhearted answers

to question who I am.

You love to inscribe "crazy"

on the reputation of volcanic women

who sacrifice eternities, dormantly devoted

to the men whose betrayal

is bursting in their cores.

You hate when I erupt with honest responses.

Like:

Lately I've caused a few hurricanes.

This is not mother nature. Nor my own.

You'll only accept the taste of deranged fruit,

when you admit to planting every seed.

As a Man Thinketh

There is no light

At the end of the tunnel.

You just do not see

The way you're glowing

In the darkness.

The end of the tunnel

Begins in your mind.

June 15, 2016

It has been one month since the abortion.

I told ███ that I'm not in love with him anymore. I said it while I was making pasta and cornbread. It sounded as passive as if I'd been talking about the weather.

I probably didn't meant it as much as I wanted a reaction from him. I do that a lot...I start fires inside of people that I care about when I need to watch them burn for me.

Well, I suppose I got what I wanted because in three moves, he showed me more emotion than he has shown our entire relationship. First, he tells me he doesn't want to talk, then he goes to the porch, then he comes in and Luther Vandross' song "Dance with My Father" is playing and he starts to cry because he misses his dad who died when he was twelve.

He said he doesn't care that I feel that way (which I don't believe) but he's upset because I've shown no signs. Also, it's impolite to just drop that on someone during dinner.

I have never seen ███ cry before. I have never felt so helpless. I wish I knew how to heal him, maybe teach him what (I think) love is. It's just that in the process, I feel used and unworthy. I'm invisible.

I thought that my love would compensate for his (lack thereof). I thought that if I held on tight enough, I could ignore the internal bleeding. If I overlooked the fact that I had to break every bone in my body to fit into his ideal mold, I would finally be worthy enough to eat from that trophy dish: the meal from which he's been plucking crumbs of his love to ration to me this whole time.

He knows that losing my confidence has made me as loyal as a stray. He only has to share just enough to make sure I'll stay around.

Even if I was always hungry, I could never say he'd starved me.

Without nourishment, I slowly disappeared. I was shrinking to make room for his insecurities. He did not care. There were no leftovers for me after he fed his ego.

Maybe it's really time to give up.

Love is Not Blind. You are.

We demand the truth...

But when their actions are the answers,

We choose to believe their words.

July 17, 2016

We went to church this morning, but we're still empty. We are sitting on a park bench amidst deterioration. There is no sun in the sky. Maybe my yellow dress suffices. Maybe I'm his sun. His sunshine. We watch the cars drive by. This is a one-way street, so they aimlessly go.

It's endless.

All of these lonely people, where do they go?

It's almost like our relationship, or what's left of it. Aimless but endless, and lonely at times.

I just asked him if he thinks our love is timeless.

He says, "Not yet."

I wish he said yes, but I know better than to hope to be lied to. Besides, I saw his phone, and he's been cheating on me again.

I know it's time for me to go.

August 16, 2016

12:44 a.m.

I just took a Clear Blue test. Again.

There is a plus sign. Again.

Three months after my last pregnancy.

I am a mother.

Again.

I think this was intentional.

Would God really give me this opportunity again? Even though I don't deserve it?

Am I still trying to replace the other one?

Or my pain?

Maybe the love that never existed.

August 22, 2016

When I told him I was pregnant again, he hung up the phone.

I am so alone.

There is nothing more that I want than to have a family, and to have to do this on my own is so heartbreaking. It is devastating. Once again—for the second time—this man leaves me with his unborn child. Last time, I thought that if I washed away his prints from inside of me, the feeling would go away. It didn't. For long periods of time, I'd catch myself staring at the clock thinking, "How much longer until this life is over?"

This time I am stronger, but it still hurts so bad. How can someone who gave me such a beautiful gift turn out to be so ugly?

I have to do this alone.

Peace, Be still

I want to walk in purpose, like I used to.

To laugh away the mornings and

Make eggs.

I want to order bromeliads from Kofi's home in Ghana

to soak in my tub tonight.

I want a wardrobe of blush lingerie

To wear, while I drink an 1888 Italian red,

and watch classics until I cry.

Not because of the kiss before the credits,

But because I know that love shit is generic.

And no man will ever throw his coat in a puddle
For my feet.

But,

I still sit in humid silence.

I forget to light the candles.

I haven't bought matches.

I still count the threads on my sheets.

I don't blink.

I create blueprints of my flaws.

I wish on 11:11 for dignity.

I sweat fevers in my sleep.

I sweat like when you gravitated inside of me,

wearing nothing but sweat.

I read the Bible.

I still don't read the Bible.

My instruments are years untuned.

My paint brushes are concrete.

This is irreparable.

I still don't give a shit.

I'm still here.

I'm still writing you letters.

Settle Down and Don't Settle

So I am promising myself to never settle.

To not become so comfortable in familiarity

That complacency is all I'll know.

I am no longer so eager

To share my soul

That I am ripping it in pieces to make room for barren promises and minimal effort.

I deserve what I demand.

So come correct.

With culture,

respect, agape love.

With lavender tea. White oleanders. Frida Kahlo.

Plane tickets.

Come with eucalyptus, bath oils, smelling like potential.

Come with theories. With pedagogy. With ideologies.

Knowing that I'll treat you like a king,

but patriarchy don't live 'round here.

And neither does assigning domesticity to gender binaries.

Wash the dishes.

Come bearing novels by the greats,

But also short, handwritten poems— by you.

Come with church.

I need you to have God on your eyelids so that I can see you praying for me.

Pray so hard that the mountains move.

That fig trees flourish.

That when my toes touch that water—

I will walk.

I need all of this.

Come and tell me that I don't look shitty,

When the baby's been crying all night.

Strum your chords through my cotton-field curls.

Appreciate the boldness of my big chop.

The eagerness of my hyperpigmentation.

The grace of these breasts that cry because they miss their milk.

For the days that I've lost strength to leave bed—

I need you to be strong enough to carry me.

To build me a new bed.

Do not patronize me.

Empathy does not make you weak.

Baptize me—

With hymns. With honey. With sunflowers.

Because you know I've got night and day confused,

But happy is on the way.

Tell me that.

That you love me,

And come with the courage to do so.

Because I may tell you the opposite.

I may break glasses,

Shatter porcelain like it's your feelings,

And talk bad about your mother.

It'll be okay, just pray for me.

And don't tell your mother.

I don't need your gifts.

I need your God.

Come bearing witness to that.

Briana Williams <bxxxxxx@jdxx.law.harvard.edu>

Mon. Jan 9, 2017, 7:57 a.m.

to gxxxxxxx4@gmail,com

I need to know whether or not you'll be coming to your baby's baby shower because I am paying PER PERSON, and I have to get the guest list together .

Sent from my iPhone

Briana Williams <bwxxxx@jdxxx.law.harvard.edu>

Mon. Jan 30, 2017, 7:19 p.m.

To: gxxxxxxxxxxxx@gmail.com

Today I went to the hospital because, for some reason, I started having contractions during class. They were so bad that I had to leave the room to throw up. And then when I went to see my doctor, they sent me to the birthing center at Mt. Auburn Hospital because they thought that I was going into preterm labor: that's when you have a premature baby. I'm almost twenty-nine weeks now though, so the baby would still be viable if born today. But thankfully that didn't happen and everything was fine. They never really told me what was wrong, but the whole thing was so scary. My dramatic ass was crying thinking I was about to have a baby today without anything prepared. I think my OCD self was most upset because I didn't even get to write the birthing plan out.

I was super tired when I got home, but I'd signed and paid up for the Newborn course from six to nine p.m., so I just came home, packed dinner, and then left. The course was so informative. I learned so many things, from sleeping and eating schedules, to how to "swaddle" the baby at night. They even taught us the sounds that most soothe the baby, how to bathe the baby, and how to detect the reason that your baby is crying. Newborns typically take at least eighteen hours per day of care. They wake up every two hours for feeding. I decided to breastfeed. When I walked into class, there were nine other couples there. I counted when I got bored. I was just thinking, "I know I'm going to cry when I get home". For every question and activity, the instructor asked the dad the same thing. Then the instructor went on a long speech about how teamwork will help everyone through the first few months. Well honestly, it's saddening that I don't have anyone by my side at these times and in these classes. I remember the first time you took me to eat on Valentine's Day, when we first met. A I was telling you how perfect that I want my baby and nursery to be, and you were just like, "It's not gonna happen all planned like that." Well, you were for sure right. But I never thought in a million years that I would be completely alone during my whole pregnancy. In a little over two months, I'll be holding our daughter, and I do not know where you will be, but I think that what you've done here is the worst thing that you can ever do to a woman.

I know you say that you wanted to get me pregnant to "fix me" because of the last one. But did you not think it through at all? Like, what would happen if I actually got pregnant? And where you'd actually be?

I hope that you will take these things into mind, because I am just so tired right now.

Brie

Self-Love When They Self-Hate

I had no space in my heart

To love myself,

While I was busy loving you.

My needs were eagerly displaced

To accommodate your emptiness.

First Loves and Spring Trees

February 24,2017

It won't be easy. It'll hit you randomly, like when you're watching *House Hunters* and a cookie cutter wife is squealing over the room that would be so "perfect for the nursery."

You'll finish that last scoop of whatever the hell it was that you know you shouldn't be eating and put yourself in her shoes.

As time progresses, it probably won't get easier. Your body is changing. The world can be mapped with the veins that have found a home in your skin. You're stretching. You will be alone to marvel at how a heart can grow inside of you, both physically and spiritually. Wait until you hear the beat for the first time. You'll cry.

You'll stop wishing he'd show up at doctor visits.

You'll ask for a 3D ultrasound—praying that your baby is all of you and none of him, because he won't even see that ultrasound.

It'll be hard, but the type of pain that has you howling at empty skies at three a.m. will not persist forever. You'll become accustomed to holding your cocoon in your sleep. You'll whisper things comparable to the greatest love known to God—things only you and your belly can know. You'll play music on top of your belly, like in the movies, and share the first dance with an angel. Bubble baths will become less lonely.

An immaculate conception. You'll respect your vessel with new eyes; you have just been given the opportunity to birth the manifestation of first loves and spring trees all in one. This is comparable to birthing the universe.

You'll figure out how to make it easier.

Briana Williams <bwilliams@jd18.law.harvard.edu>

Tues. April 11, 2017, 8:08 PM

to gxxxxxxxxxxx4@gmail.com

So how am I going to call you for labor when I'm blocked?

She is due next week...........

3:49 p.m.

September 14, 2017—Thursday

I overlooked you leaving me alone during labor, crying so hard that the doctors were alerted to my hyperventilating because it tampered with the baby's air supply. They made me take Benadryl.

I overlooked that I had to buy you a ticket to meet her when she was three-months-old, and you used it as a vacation, visiting the house only a few times.

I didn't even stay mad that I'd been sleep deprived into delirium because breastfeeding every two hours for months turned my nights into mornings. Every day.

Instead, I wanted a "real" family so bad that I practically begged you to come back.

So you came to Cambridge, unapologetically and unemployed, smelling like cheap perfume and entitlement.

And I can tell that you are not happy.

You don't have the patience for this five-month-old baby who prefers her mother.

You barely look at me.

I can cook. I can clean. I can dream, love, smile, and breathe warmth down your spine. I can move to Egypt. I can move a mountain. I can be wind, a Nashville eclipse,

God.

But your eyes are void of hearing as if you do not remember. You'd rather other women's words give you something to look forward to. My sweet "nothings" are palliatives. They don't scratch the surface of what seems to be an impenetrable aversion to my advances. I am lonely, deprived, and insecure.

Why did you even come back?

I am realizing that I will never be the one you choose. I'm not okay with that,

But maybe one day I won't mind.

September 20, 2017

I don't know when I realized that I am impossible to love.

Maybe it was during the time Alex abandoned me, or when ▮▮▮ didn't show up for our daughter's birth.

I cut her umbilical cord.

Maybe flowers

Soaked in honeypots

Are an acquired taste.

Maybe they're no longer in style.

But somewhere entrenched in this revelation,

I've accepted some form of existential angst and defeatism that probably prevents me from loving, too.

Maybe Cornel West's nihilistic pedagogy resonated into my reality.

Because compliments are not flattering unless they tumble from tongues that have

cursed me.

That is called redemption.

Hugs are not love unless they suffocate me.

That is called passion.

That is called crazy.

Last night I dreamt that Richard wrote me letters.

He was searching for my smile—for old times' sake.

So this morning I walked past the postman—his wave brought a flicker of memories that I've suppressed (well enough)

To the surface.

I thought of how I sent him

A cake. A map. A book. Books. Photos. Letters. Words. Me. My soul. A blueprint to my soul.

You know, with all the mazes? Had me looking like a scarecrow.

And when he chose her, he packed all those things up,

Leaving the blood-stained, cardboard box

(dripping with honey suckle) at my doorstep.

They were home...

My love had come home—'cause it belongs to no one.

I cannot be loved.

September 21, 2017

Today I asked ███ to write a list of ten things

He loves about me.

I told myself that if he couldn't list ten, I'd never love him again.

But for the issue that he could list only five for himself—I would have kept that promise.

Because he only listed nine.

So, what most agitates me is that he used all

ADJECTIVES.

Yet on the list of the ten things that he hates, he used

Full sentences.

Grammar. Pronouns. All that shit—I was shook!

I kind of don't care though.

Remember, he doesn't

Even love

Himself

(enough).

I Don't Want Your Spare Change

You are the hope that

drowns in those fountains

that won't ever stop

Lusting for my pennies

But never intend to satisfy

My Wishes.

Addicts Love to Visit their Attics

On dry occasions,

Such as rainy days...

When our moments collect dust.

In the attic of my recollection,

I will thumb through your memories

Like old photographs,

Placing your smile in a

Frame of perfection

And imagine.

If you'd have chosen me.

What we could've

Been.

Love's Labor

I'm pregnant with self-doubt.

I birth pain,

But his love is still

Inconceivable.

Juice

Mayo told me that

What sets me apart

Is that no one can outwork me.

I won't stop.

The Apple(s) of Your Eye(s)

I have <u>hated</u> women

Who I've never had the pleasure

Of knowing.

Because you were so willing

To pay them *any* price

For things that I gave you—for free.

October 18, 2017

I wake up in the mornings and drink coffee that is straight from San Antonio, Texas. By this time, Evelyn has probably been babbling for about an hour or so. I read. I check my email and social media. Today I threw a load in the dryer. We went to the park. A few meetings. I read some more. Tonight I plan to read, attend a dinner hosted by The Women's Law Association, put away the laundry. I'll make vegetable soup from the herbs that I brought from Turkey and give Evie a bath that is full of Turkish rose petals.

I hope that I have the courage and energy to attend to all of these things. I am tired. Simultaneously, restless.

Yesterday was my birthday. I realized that my therapist is pretty useless. She's only probably good for behavioral-enhancing meds. All of the emotional tactics and behavioral modifications that she suggests, I already implement. My birthday was uneventful and disappointing. ▮ did not as much as send me a flower. This was a turning point in my perception of the relationship.

It made me toy with the idea of spending the rest of my life not getting roses.

Not receiving grand, romantic gestures without pressure. A love removed of spontaneity and spring. I became disengaged and lost interest in trying to celebrate my birthday. Though I was unable to identify it at the time, I'm aware that my sadness stems from the disconnected romance to which I am an accomplice.

Will I always settle? I mean, am I settling? Or is this the greatest love of all time?

I don't burn for him like I used to, but maybe it is, as my therapist describes, "part of our pendulum." What does she know?

Regardless, I do not care to be complicit in a half- burning love affair. I need fresh linens. Volcanic lovemaking. Cotton-field touches. I need the galaxy backing me on this.

I plan to find this.

I Think My Past Is Unresolved

When I'm drunk, I cry (for myself).

A lot. I cry about feeling like an inadequate mother.

Maybe my daughter won't remember,

But she'll internalize my selfish passion.

I cry because

My mother

Was the first person that made me realize

That I was ugly.

And I carried that stain on my soul

Into adulthood. Then burned it in the beds of men

Who didn't deserve me.

But at least they called me pretty.

I sent you this text at 12:07 p.m.

August 2018

Look at us. Look at what we have done. How did we get here?

This is an apology letter to the both of us

For how long it took me to let things go.

I could've sworn you needed me

Like I needed you. But this is

Really killing me. I have never wanted to die so much as I

Have sitting in the basement

Alone and cold, crying.

The other day I seriously considered asking you to be with me and telling you that I would allow you to also be with other women. I thought about offering you threesomes. I balanced being able to have at least part of you and felt that it was worth it. You are my first love. You are the only man that I wanted to marry, to have all of my children with. To grow old with— and make love to eternally.

I realize that even that will not change what we both know. I cannot have a death grip on someone that does not belong to me. This entire time I have been fighting for you. Fighting with you. Fighting alone because you are so disconnected, it's like you do not see me. This morning, I told you I would wait for you, and I meant it. But I know that is not what you want. You can't commit to that—I felt in in your throat.

I am so sorry. I cannot agonize anymore over not being good enough for you. I can't keep killing myself; my spirit is so heavy, I feel like I am dying. I know that I need to let you go so that we can both be happy, I just hadn't had the strength to do so.

It's time. I cannot pour over your social media. I cannot stomach your messages. I gave you all I've got and I've got nothing left. I want you to be happy. I will work on myself and try to be better for you and Evelyn. I feel so weak. Please pray for me. I feel so broken.

I am ready to let you go, and I am sorry for suffocating you to keep you.

Broken Wings

I eat because weeks without food can make even Ghandi a bit delusional. It takes effort to breathe. Every night I can remember putting Evelyn to bed...my nightingale...but I never remember sleeping. Just wine-induced slumber and red-stained lips that beg my ex for reasons not even religion can unmask.

Interlude

It's over. We are done. Are we really? Let it be so. Every time we try to repair the destruction, we end up worse than before. I am tired of being cheated on. I am tired of what cheating does to my mirror; it's so dishonest these days. I'm constantly begging it to explain to me why I am not good enough for loyalty, and it only wants to show me someone that I swore to never become. There's no way that I look like that. That's how I know you don't hate me. You just can't recognize me, either. You just hate the echo of your lies.

Maybe I will give it a couple of years. Would that be enough time for a clean slate? For me to track down my innocence? For me to stop having to look over my shoulder and compete with a hundred "I swear I don't know her(s)"?

Will you become a stranger? I do not want to share my daughter with a stranger. I ache at the thought of you getting another woman pregnant and her experiencing everything that I feel like I was robbed of. I do not know if I have honestly forgiven you. I cannot let it go. Belly-touching photos, a gender reveal, a baby shower—really any form of celebrating new life. Don't.

Will you run to the store for her three a.m. cravings? It would kill me.

Will my womb watch in agony? Will I live vicariously through your family portraits, placing my face on hers and immersing myself in the secluded delusion of us being whole?

I am glad the world has enjoyed my stories about you. To me, they were not beautiful nor interesting. They were a bit therapeutic, but mostly, they were pain. I am happy that my audience can enjoy my pain.

Part II

From: Trying to find another you knowing that I needed to find me first.

To: The lover's time that I must be wasting.

I lost myself back there,

so I need you to handle my soul

as the bee does the flower:

Take all of my honey,

but do not leave me withered.

To: Dyer's "Michichi"

CC: Michichi DeDios

Maybe I deserve this suffering,

But I am sick enough to admit that I find comfort in knowing that—

Though he chose you,

Your womb will always be forced to waltz with my ghost.

Your ultimatum for his returning home was that he give you his gospel.

"Tell me the truth."

It must be agonizing to hear the holiness in each syllable of my name.

To read my anatomy in his hymn books and understand why he loves communion

so much.

I am his Sunday morning.

I thought about giving you an apology.

But all that he's confessed to me is buried in your sheets.

Let's call it even.

To: My Memory

I love when the rain is violent because it gives me an excuse to be lonely. I relax in the white jacket of memories my heart's asylum refers to as crazy. I can test my capacity to feel: If dandelion tea burns my tongue—at least my organs are loyal.

I can convince myself that it is no longer painful to stumble upon the juncture of sun rays and Georgia peaches:

his smile.

Or the painting of it that I keep locked in my subconscious.

I can't sleep anymore these days because of the noisiness.

It's not New York's insomniac streets.

The walls of my apartment whisper too loud.

They're tired of watching me curled up in sweat, tired of my prayers getting trapped in their wallpaper.

They complain that there is never any sunlight anymore.

They believe I should open the window,

but I can't.

I hate the moon's hypocrisy.

It taunts me,

flaunting that the man that I love, the one who never chose me, breathes underneath the same sky as I do.

Even my hands complain that I mistake them for the oceanside, all the salt water tears

that I plant in their palms.

To: Kat's Lover

Every man was a book.

And you know these are interesting books to read…

But You.

You were a poem:…

Short and meaningful.

You were never very confident.

Your spinal cord did not carry the austere of paper transfixed to a binder.

You did not make the kind of impression on history that leads to coffee houses and forever.

But you stole my imagination.

Your lies were the ballpoints whose ink carved love into my skin like razors.

You know what you did.

You know that your words perched themselves like lullabies on the circumference of my windpipes.

They ate into my flesh like starving beasts would a fresh corpse.

They danced on decaying pages,

To the music of my desperation.

Clearly you were not a love poem.

There were no mushy illustrations or cliché nothings about the way my heart reacted to your pores.

Those butterflies became batted creatures,

clawing at the pit of my stomach. Stuck somewhere between, "I know better," and "I need more."

Sorry that I couldn't stop praying for your timelessness.

I went to poetry houses just to find your vibe.

I hid your incompetence inside of me like a bookmark.

I was only trying to make happy endings make sense.

I know you saw past that.

You knew that I was just the awkward girl,

sitting at the edge of a skyline,

writing drunk letters that I am too afraid to mail to your house.

Sorry for writing you this love story.

To: Matthew 11:28

I offer you this burden:

I need to get some sleep.

I stay up to read his old texts.

They're so beautifully unrealistic

that they strip the skin off of every wound he left.

You Lusted This Love

It wasn't love.

You only wanted to experience

How it feels to lie in a bed of roses.

Baby, it feels like kissing thorns.

Leave me again, so I can remind you.

To: Joey

CC: Craazysexiicool

I don't remember the last time I've danced like that. I found God in these ruins, and I loved him fierce...So much that I ran through San Juan, harmonizing my skin like I was pandering with the beat of cobblestoned streets and ice cold Coronas.

I had forgotten how it felt to have worries smaller than butterfly wings.

To have my fingers make pinky promises with the air. I forgot blue. I forgot the sky. I forgot the shiver of sensuality that the stroke of a paintbrush, or the humming of piano keys, sent up my spine.

And now my body's trembling because it's starting to remember.

I only wanted to kick my legs up and dance in foreign places and hunt jungles with sugar cane dripping off of my tongue, so that's exactly what I did.I took my platoon, and I played Queen.

I just didn't know it would feel so good.

I didn't know that I was giving my life up, that there was an overbearing shadow, just outside my windowsill. That it lurked through the walls of my bedroom and intertwined itself in my linen. I didn't know that love would seep itself into the fragility of my fractured bones. That it would start in the summertime with kisses on my porch, between the inhalation of a few cigarettes, and end at the beginning of winter, with my dislocated jaw and police trudging on that very same porch.

I'm pretty sure that I found joy when I realized that it's supposed to come in small bundles.

To me, it came in the form of life and courage. Of self-discipline and understanding. It came with respect.

I fell for it, so it came for me.

And now I'm dancin'. I'm dancin' like the joy had never left the soles of my toes and it feels good.... It feels so damn good.

I'm dancing to Marte's song, and it feels so damn good.

To: Us Strangers

I know what it feels like to look in the mirror and not recognize yourself.

I know what it feels like to live inside of an illusion. We are nakedly parading around the masquerade. I am uncrossing my legs while seductively staring depression in the eyes.

I know what it is to lose. And then to style this fancy skeleton to strut down catwalks, shoulder to shoulder with numb paradoxes that hunger for dreams yet regurgitate reality. And their insides.

Those that thirst for answers, but swallow confusion in the form of alcoholic remedies and other people's bullshit.

Really, we're all just piling on the make-up so that we can do regular, daily things...things like floss and drink tea in the mornings;I do those things now too...I mean, yesterday I even did my laundry. Like snow, I floated in between the blank spaces in my life and folded clothes. I drifted to the same place that he'd left me: irreparable— we'd broken into a million pieces of glass. No matter how much blood gushed through the cuts, I kept trying to put us back together.

The worst part is, I don't have anything to show for it but a vague memory of who I was. I am watching my life drift away, not seeing a thing.

I know what it feels to wake up and not recognize who you are.

To not feel time escaping through the threads in your palms or the anchors in your fingertips.

To not smell sunflowers and to not feel the burn of coffee when it romances the cigarettes you've just purged in your lungs.

Don't worry.

One day, you will wake up and remember why you loved that freckle right beneath your nose. Or how much you adored the soft curve of your lashes...Nana's lashes.

You'll realize that it had nothing to do with that person. That you were beautiful in the first place, like before they ever told you...Because they didn't even invent those words, you know...

Actually,

they didn't even invent shit.

You'll learn to love yourself again.

Interlude

All the loves

I ever had,

But I only smile

At the thought

Of the only one

That killed me.

Part III- Mellifera's Mantras

I never wrote them love poems

I do not write love poems.

These memories are eulogies.

The sweetest honey in the world,

May have lived on my tongue, but I've never tasted it.

Because nothing could ever be sweeter than

The memory of he, who

I am missing.

Reminder Re: Unproductive Relationships

If it does not serve my body, intellect, or soul,

I will not allow it or subscribe to it.

Whether it be negativity, gossip, people, sustenance, music—anything.

I am not a vessel for despondency,

Nor am I willing to carry it for others.

I am

Protective of my peace

And of my well-being.

If you cannot adhere to this,

You cannot be a part of my

Space.

Intimacy

Everything is so digitized.

Nothing feels intimate anymore.

Don't text me.

Write me a letter.

Anxiety

"Where do I fly

to get out of my skin"?

I Need Me More

♪♪
♪♪
I   can   be   selfish   with   my   time.   ♪♪
I've   got   things   to   do.♪♪
Sometimes   I   cannot   be   available   ♪♪
To   anyone   other   than   myself.♪♪
I   am   okay   with   that.♪
♪

Move

You are your biggest hurdle.

Once you finally realize that,

There will be nothing that you cannot

Move.

Social Media

Stop watching other people's journeys and letting their narratives make you feel discouraged about your current chapter.

Their purpose does not compare to yours. ten times out of ten, they're only showing you the prettiest parts of their process anyways.

You're not on their time.

You've made your own.

Pick your soul up and move accordingly.

Babylon

It's understandable to want to be loved.

But do not let that desire mean that you are cheating yourself.

Do not lower your standards for the "love" of someone who you know isn't for you.

Who cannot even speak your love language.

Won't even learn it.

It's better to be lonely than to fill those gaps with

Emptiness.

Your Mirror Holds The Greatest Love Story Ever Told

There are people out there who will prey on your desire to be loved.

They will use it to manipulate you into thinking that they, who could never measure, are the best you can do. Have you thinking that "no one will ever love you like [they] can."

There is someone who can love you better than they

Ever could:

You.

Be an Ultimatum

They treat you like this because

They are not afraid to

Lose you.

But if you keep letting them,

you will lose yourself.

If no one else will, you need to have the courage

To choose you.

Lurking pt. 2

I have places to go. I can't keep searching backwards.

Omega

Tell me you love me...

With a room full to the sky

Of balloons.

Blush, pink balloons.

And/or white roses.

Say less.

Be tender with me.

You want a girl that you can

"chase" because you think you've disguised your

Subscription to patriarchy with

An "old school swag" and "chivalry."

I'm uninterested.

In all three of those concepts—

And four—including you.

If I have to blanket my cravings with elusiveness

Just to keep you eager.

I'm just too unfiltered for that.

Too music.

Too raw.

I'm not afraid to look you in your face

And tell you that

I want you.

And I'd like for you to want me

Right back.

Stop trying to chase me.

Those chases get less enticing with every catch.

Use that energy

To reciprocate

My tenderness.

Hey Bighead

You waited until I was

Deaf

To tell me all the things

I begged

To hear.

Mary Never Married

I am tired of using my hair to

wash the feet of men

That continue to walk all over me,

Before they run

Out of desire to stay.

Lurking

Stop pretending it's about closure.

There's no reason to revisit those damned places.

Briana's Blueprint

If you loved me,

You wouldn't waste your time on

Materialism.

You'd shower me with

Books by James Baldwin

(preferably *The Price of the Ticket*, which I don't have yet).

You'd plant flowers in the living room,

Because that's not where they belong.

We do not always belong.

You'd pour sugar on my words,

So you could taste my intentions.

You'd know me.

Quicksand

You're not going to move forward

Unless

You let go.

Seems simple,

But it's like diving into a pool of rejection.

Like being baptized in the tears of a liar.

The liar that you love.

Stop swimming in broken promises,

Just because you can open your eyes underwater.

Give yourself a chance to come up for air.

Sorry Amigo

Why do you wear that mask?

Are you not more than your name?

Than your knowledge?

Than your skin?

Than your skin against my skin?

Maybe I am not what you

Want,

But I am what you

Need.

Strip you bare, and I'm still here.

I want to see how naked

You can be with clothes on.

Trust me, I'll choose your soul.

Every.

Single.

Time.

Generational Violence

Most fractures don't hurt me.

My jaw didn't hurt.

The bruises always fade.

Real pain was when my daughter touched my tears

Exploratively.

Like she didn't understand how

Water could sing to her songstress.

She was cautious.

Then she started to cry, too.

Real pain was knowing that

She cried

Because she understood my pain.

And there was nothing that I could do about it.

A Blues for Shuana

I want a love that looks

Like fresh roses

And feels like a

Nina record.

That tastes like

The mind of a first kiss.

That smells like lemongrass,

In the South,

In the morning.

That ages indefinitely,

But never grows old.

You Better Give Me Everything

There's the man that will buy you your favorite bottle of wine.

And there's the man that will build you the vineyard.

With his bare hands.

No more settling.

Prayers to Those Who Are Our Prayers

It's always the people that are so much of a light to the world

Who do not know how to fight

Their own darkness.

Pray for that friend you lean on.

They're hurting, just like you.

The only difference is, is that—

Threaded in their smile—

They carry everyone else's pain

With their own.

Jealousy is Why I Never Left

Could you admit that

The only reason that you

Allow yourself to continue to suffer

In your current relationship

Is because—not the thought of the person moving on—

The thought of them giving someone else everything that you deserve...

Everything that you've lost yourself over...

Kills you.

Let Them Be

If you pour life into someone

And they take

Without reciprocating—it's because

They are not qualified to.

The next relationship won't make them any more

Qualified.

Them being with someone else is not going to make them

Fulfill the potential that you see in them.

The potential is who YOU thought you could build them to be.

They are not that person.

They will give the next person the same (if not more) insufferable qualities—

That is who they are.

I Will Attract What I Demand (I Will Keep What I Accept)

1. I demand a lover

     a. whose kisses caress places human kisses cannot go.

     b. who plants seeds of witness in the crevices of my brokenness

     c. who hums boldness to the hollows of my shame

     d. who cleanses my aches with amnesia (so that I may forget to dwell in the damage while God reminds me who I am).

Toy Soldier

Stop giving everyone access to you.

To your home. Your sanity.

You'll self-destruct going to war for people

Who wouldn't even step on the

Field for you.

No More Funeral Sex and Graveyard Visits

I believe in Goodbye.

This cannot be mournful.

My Dahlias belong in the protection

Of a man—

Who deserves me.

Not at the

Bedside of a

Toxic lover.

Not on the grave of a

Dead relationship.

4:06 a.m.

I think that God broke my heart to save my life.

Bolaji

We prayed today.

Bolaji said she saw angels camped around me. She said not to conform. She said that I can resist without conceding. She reminds me of "LIVE" faith that's been lost in the pastures of vanity.

And I relate so much to Vanity, because I've never stopped searching for the prince (not in *Purple Rain,* but both in heaven and on Earth). You know baby?

She reminds me of how we should appreciate the ones who listen more than they speak. She listens.

She inspired me to

Tell you guys that:

This is my last poem to you.

I haven't lived in your home. I've not drank from your well, but I've found you. I loved you with the loyalty of Rachel, the devastation of Leah, and the dumbfoundedness of Jacob. I found love in the way that you have dug up the pain in your core because my experience with life mirrors your gravity. I get it. We get it.

My last poem to you wants you to know that:

You are the poem.

You are my poem. If you don't dig up your pain and take it to war, you will lose your soul under the quilts of modulation. Really, you've never stopped trying to make sense of how to love you after "they, it, or you" made you feel less than you really are.

Be your own favorite poem. You are the author of the never-ending story.

Stop trying to erase. Hold your book like it's the prayer before communion and the script to your last dance. Use it to

Demand your next series.

The best is yet to come.

Psalms 91.

August 1, 2010.

God Will Rise

My soul is shaken. The streets crumble in pain.

When I say that they took one of ours, I do not mean it phenotypically.

I mean, I knew who you belonged to when you showed the world proof that there is a God

Merely by existing.

I Will Never Stop Loving Him

Love is never lost. Each chapter of our love stories prepares us for our happy ending. I am grateful to have loved strongly enough to both lay down my life and create a new one. I look forward to experiencing how it feels to love someone else when I truly love and know myself.

Forgiveness

Endings are never promised,

so always place your hope

In a better beginning.

You can begin,

Anywhere you want.

Go.

In the end,

I survived.

Then I survived the me that you created.

That is what

Matters the most.

My Beginning.

Made in United States
Orlando, FL
16 June 2024